fancy plastic bags

Written By

Brynn Arendt
Katrina De Man
Lori Cook
Julie Pearson

fancy plastic bags

Giving Our Daughters More

pot-boilers

Requests for permission should be made in writing to:
Pot-Boilers, 100 Stevens St. SW, Grand Rapids, MI 49507

www.pot-boilers.com

Book jacket design & layout by Deksia Design LLC.

ISBN 13 / 978-0-578-10319-8

Manufactured in the United States of America
1 2 3 56 78 23 23 11

contents

Introduction

Four inches.

Four inches that brought my dreams to life. But those dreams were almost transformed into nightmare.

The hours spent in bridal shops had reached a level of excess. The prices of the new gowns seemed ludicrous. What were a weary bride-to-be and her ever loving, wedding-dress-shopping mother to do? Of course, I did find a new dress that captured my heart – but not my father's wallet.

The bridal store owner noticed my affinity for the too-expensive dress. Out of pure altruism she put me in contact with a recent bride who had worn the same dress just two months earlier.

So I called her.

I know. Can you believe I had the nerve? What new bride wants to pry her sticky manicured nails off of pure, white satin? But if there was a morsel of a chance that she would sell, I had to know.

I cringed as I asked, bracing myself for rejection. But as we talked, she relayed that a few weeks earlier she felt led to make changes in her relationship to material possessions. So when

I called to ask, she was ready to be open-handed with her wedding dress.

We arranged a meeting in the locker room of a sports facility. I tried on her dress. It fit perfectly, with the exception of being too long – four inches too long. In other words, totally workable. And the price? A fraction of the original price. My dreams had new life.

This story still stuns me. The elegance and creativity of that dress was all that I'd hoped for in a wedding dress. It was unusual, but tasteful. Modest, yet interesting. I loved it. And now it was mine because of the unbelievable giving of a stranger. Her kindness still stands as an example to me.

But here's the thing. That dress? I took it off after my wedding reception and put it in one of those fancy, plastic dress bags. It's still there, and hasn't been removed since. While my story is still spectacular, that beautiful dress lives unused and untouched in a fancy plastic bag.

God has designed our daughters with unique, inner beauty, and He doesn't want that beauty to be lost underneath a fancy, plastic veneer. As a mom, you're the person best equipped to draw out your daughter's femininity and help shape her into a woman of God. And as you pour your love and influence into her, God is also working to shape you.

As women, we have unique abilities to generate life, touch hearts and powerfully influence. And we long to do all of those things with our girls. But what does that look like – and why is it often so confusing? How do we navigate through the minefields in today's culture? How do we press on when we're drop-dead weary or when our daughters seem to want *us* to drop dead?

The pages you hold contain stories from moms at all stages of life, practical ideas and everyday opportunities to influence your daughter.

Because in the end, we want to give our daughters more than fancy, plastic-coated femininity.

Season 01: Generate

Birth to 5 Years

Author: Brynn Arendt

Most of Brynn's best moments are spent listening to her rock star husband play the drums and reading to her four inquisitive children. She enjoys strolling outdoors absorbing the delights that Michigan's four seasons have to offer, and has a lifelong goal of memorizing the Mid West's common bird calls. She has degrees in Psychology and Leadership and is employed in Children's Ministry and Adult Education at a local University.

HAD I FAILED?

Before my husband and I celebrated our sixth anniversary, we had a minivan complete with four car seats and a booger bar, a living room that resembled a shrine to medium-sized plastic objects that jiggled smiles onto babies' faces, a wardrobe that now had clothing several sizes bigger than those I wore a few years back (many of the pants with 18 inches of elastic wrapped around the top) and four kids. When strangers asked me what I did for a living, I told them the truth: "I'm a professional wiper."

The only popular songs I knew came from *VeggieTales* DVDs. I had all of the Dr. Seuss books memorized. For five years straight, I wore the same pair of earrings and never wore eye makeup. I loved Halloween because the permanent display of cobwebs inside and outside my house made me feel like I had festively decorated for the holiday. I was addicted to coffee. And when I went to the end of the driveway to get the mail, I pretended I was going away by myself on a three-month vacation to Fiji.

When my youngest daughter turned three, I was talking with another mother about how unbelievable – truly unbelievable – it was to me that my kids survived their early years. But it was even more shocking that I had survived their early years. I expressed how wild it was to feel that way. It wasn't like I had just survived being lost at sea or anything so horrible. Her immediate response to me was, "Well, it kind of *is* like being lost at sea. You know, having young kids can almost kill you."

Here's an excerpt from my journal the day I was told my second child was going to be a girl.

January 7, 2002

My little girl,

Even as I write to you – just 28 weeks inside me! – I feel your feet kick against the wall of protection that surrounds you. You have intrigued me so as you remain ever committed to staying on the right side of my tummy. Your brother was all over the place when I carried him, but you have remained consistently tucked in the corner you prefer.

I want you to know it is a joy to carry you inside me. There are countless women who long to be able to carry a baby inside, but cannot. I know you are a gift to me and I am so thankful I have been given the blessing of being your mom.

There are some important things I want you to know, and I will continue to explain them as you grow older. I need you to know you can come to me when you are in need of something. When you are hungry, I will feed you. When you are cold, I will warm you up. When you are wet, I will dry you. When you are tired, I will sing a lullaby and rock you to sleep. And when you are scared, I will pray for you and wrap my arms around your precious body.

I will do all these things, and more, as long as you need me to, but also because that is what I was made to do. And the reason I can do these things for you is because I have had these things done for me.

When my soul is hungry, He feeds me. When I am cold with loneliness, He pursues. When I am uncomfortable, He assures me. When I am tired, He lifts me up. When I am scared, He wraps His promises all the way around me.

And, you see, my daughter, you were created to give these things away to others as well. I will teach you what it means to give life to those in need and together we will seek the One who has given life to us.

~ Mom

That little one is now almost 11 years old. All those years, I have kept the commitment I made to her while in the womb.

Except that day during my third pregnancy when my bones were screaming with fatigue and I cried in the front seat of the car and could only whisper to my husband, "The only thing I know is exhaustion."

Or that other time when I was scared about how we were going to afford major repairs on both cars, and it was Christmas time, and I had just spilled an entire cup of coffee on our MacBook, and my husband was leaving the country for a month. To cope with my fears, I didn't share a tea bag with my sister.

And then there was the day when I hungered so badly for order in my house that I yelled at my two-year-old daughter for throwing all her snotty tissues on the bathroom floor next to the trashcan rather than in the trashcan. She cried.

Or how about when we lived in a residence hall with 350 college students and I was mega pregnant and walking in from a far-away parking lot carrying a sleeping toddler and I got mad because, despite the masses, no one opened the door to the building for me. When I got into our apartment my anger blinded me from remembering to raise the side on my toddler's crib. When I left the room she woke up. And fell out.

Remember my journal letter? How I promised to dry my wet child when she was in need? How do you think I was feeling about that promise when I started counting? Counting diapers – 16 changes in one day. Cloth diapers.

Had I failed?

I think my journal writing is super sweet, but that's all it is. I had no idea how my need for growth would surface in the challenges ahead. When the babies are coming and toddlers are weeble-wobbling all through the house, a mom often feels there is no life to give.

My friend couldn't be right, could she? Will having young kids almost kill me?

As always, knowing our story – the story of woman – is helpful.

WE ARE GENERATORS

Woman was created and named Eve – mother of all living things. Her body was shaped beautifully and specifically for carrying and sustaining life, something man was never made to do. But biological life was not the only life she was meant to offer. Relationally, her tenderness would create an emotional sensitivity that would allow others to flourish in her safety. All of this was a reflection of the God who made her. A God who creates, sustains and blesses relationships.

Then the world broke and all that was created no longer resembled its design. Everything became gnarled and twisted and woman's ability to cultivate life was wrought with pain, selfishness and failure.

But then came the promise of regeneration, of life coming from what was lost, broken, and dead. That promise was made in a person – our Savior – and woman once again had hope. Hope of knowing Him and allowing Him to transform the brokenness into beauty.

Despite the trials and failures, we are still called to be life givers and to find joy in the process. The process of generating life into our daughters, who can then, in turn, generate life into others.

As mothers of baby girls, this process begins early. As early as the first breath.

Many scientific studies have confirmed that we are born with a preference for sights and sounds that facilitate social responsiveness. Newborns consistently turn their heads toward the sound of human voices and gaze longer at a drawing of a face-like image as opposed to an image with a bull's-eye pattern on it. Newborns prefer to look at objects 8 to 12 inches away

– which is just the distance between a nursing baby's eyes and the eyes of its mother! The mother's smell is stamped in the baby's brain within days so that, if placed between the scent of its mother on a gauze pad and the scent of another woman on a different gauze pad, a baby will usually turn toward the smell of its own mother. If recordings of the mother's voice are played alongside the voice of another woman, the baby will suck more vigorously on its pacifier when it hears the sounds of its own mom.[1]

These studies are telling us that children, from birth, are designed to receive the bonding initiatives of mothers. And those bonding initiatives in turn produce attachment. The next time you are at a day care center or church nursery, check out the one-year-olds when their moms pick them up to go home. The scene is full of wild hugs and kisses. There is no other social behavior more striking than the intense and mutual infant-parent bond.

What forms attachment in infants? Two things. The first is physical contact. Infants become attached to women who are soft and warm and rock and pat and snuggle and feed and clothe and sing and smile to their babies. The second is familiarity. Infants become attached to what they know. The mere exposure to familiar people and things (such as books, traditions and foods) fosters fondness.

So how do we connect this with our call, as mothers, to generate life into our infant daughters? In a word, our baby girls need our time. They need us holding them and rocking them and singing to them and snuggling with them and kissing them and zurburting them. And they need it all over again the next day and the next day…

This will produce in an infant the psychological and social capacity to trust and enjoy strong relationships some day. When our children are babies, we invest the time to form an attachment with them so that as they grow and mature they can receive and extend this generating power. This early groundwork knits the soul so that one day our baby becomes a woman who can bless and heal and lead and think and love and serve those around her.

What an opportunity! Annie Sullivan once said, "It is a rare privilege to watch the birth, growth, and first feeble struggles of a living human mind."[2] The mother's viewpoint is a front row seat into the marvelous development of baby to adult. We are crucial to the success of it all. How highly does our Creator think of our motherly influence!

But what happens when you don't have all this time for zurburting? What if you have lots of toddlers and piles of laundry and deadlines at work? What if you actually try to cook dinner at night for your family and shower every three days? How is all of this managed? How do we foster a long-term vision of generating life into our daughters when we feel we have nothing left inside to work with?

I understand your angst. Sadly, I had to learn by hurting my kids before finding the answers.

KEEP. THEM. ALIVE.

Each day when I wake up, a list begins to stream through the big screen of my vision. On the list are things like: unload dishwasher, collect husband's dirty socks from crevices under sofa, wipe finger prints off refrigerator and windows, wipe dust bunnies out of corners, bake banana bread, listen to cultural commentaries on radio, run three miles and read Shakespeare. Accomplishing these things, especially if done so by 6:30am, is something I find thrilling.

The problem comes when it's 8:30am and I haven't accomplished any of the things on my list and all of my kids are awake early looking at me with hungry eyes. This was particularly a problem when my kids were babies and toddlers. They were always pooping, spitting up and crying at times when I wanted to accomplish things on my list. How did I respond? I got angry. I was angry at not having the thrill of checking things off my list. This was such a problem that I knew I needed to make some drastic changes. So I changed my list.

Every time I had a baby, I allowed myself only one thing on my list. That was the only thing on the list until my baby was three months old. What was it? "Keep Children Alive." That was it - for the first three months of every one of my children's lives. The only thing I had to do every day was keep my children alive. If I started to feel angry at the end of the day because I hadn't finished the laundry, I would remind myself that "completing laundry" was not on my list. If I felt tremendous guilt because my kids had watched the Baby Einstein video for three hours straight, I would look at my list and realize "mental stimulation of children" was not on my list. If I looked in the mirror before my husband came home from work and shrieked at my reflection, I would remind myself that "look amazing" was not on my list. But when I tucked my kids into bed at night and heard each of their soft breathing patterns, I knew I had accomplished everything on my list.

After three months, I allowed myself to add one more thing to the list. Maybe I would add, "cook dinner." This strategy gave me freedom as I slowly reached the place where I could expect more productivity from my day.

But guess what happened during those first few months of list shrinking? My energetic, thrill-seeking self began to crave less the rush of "being on top of it" and instead began to crave the generation of life in my babies and toddlers. I lost the task-driven distraction and instead found that time spent with kids on my lap reading books and singing lullabies and counting marbles won my heart. I found that when I gave my mother's heart fully to my little ones, I was generating in them a security that far, far outweighed their appreciation for clear counter tops. I was, in the truest sense of the word, being productive in the most righteous sense of the word. I was discovering the deep joy of motherhood – joy that is meant to flow into others and generate life.

GUARANTEED FRUSTRATION

The bottom line with this topic, and all other topics out there, is that we will always be tempted to go our own way to make life work. For me, it was (and still is) that feeling of being on top of it all. Each day I must face that desire, repent, and ask God to renew my energy and vision as a woman and mother.

How are you most often tempted? Toward a life of ease and pleasure, where your children are distanced so they don't complicate your plans? Toward a life of consumption, where full closets give the illusion of a full life? Toward a life of emotional entanglement, where your security lies in the feeling of closeness you have with others, including your children?

However we try to carve out life on our own terms, this promise is certain: that way will be frustrated. God loves us too much. He so values our role as a mother that He will not let us find success in wrong directions. And if you have the blessing of His Spirit in your life, you will be gently prompted to repent of that way and follow a truer, more life-giving path. A path that is more about God, and less about you.

C.S. Lewis wrote in *Mere Christianity*:

> *That is, I think, one little part of what Christ meant by saying that a thing will not really live unless it first dies. It is simply no good trying to keep any thrill: that is the very worst thing you can do. Let the thrill go – let it die away – go through that period of death into the quieter interest and happiness that follow – and you will find you are living in a world of new thrills all the time....*[3]

As women we were made to lead and offer thrilling lives to our daughters. But not the kind of thrills created by our culture. Those thrills are way too small and short-lived. Allow those to die, and what waits can take our breath away.

GIVING OUR DAUGHTERS MORE – SEASON 1

1. Engage in physical contact with your baby regularly and extensively.
2. Redefine "productivity". Pray for a realistic and authentic definition, and embrace it.
3. Let laundry pile up if it results in more bonding time with your infant.

Season 02: Study

Age 5-10

Author: Brynn Arendt

Most of Brynn's best moments are spent listening to her rock star husband play the drums and reading to her four inquisitive children. She enjoys strolling outdoors absorbing the delights that Michigan's four seasons have to offer, and has a lifelong goal of memorizing the Mid West's common bird calls. She has degrees in Psychology and Leadership and is employed in Children's Ministry and Adult Education at a local University.

MY 5K NIGHTMARE

The winds were gusting to 30mph. Temperatures in the low 30's. Ideal conditions for a January board game night. Not so much for a 5K run in the first week of May. My children, who had slept in their clothes in hopes of making the transition from warm bed to cold car easier, began slumping out of bed at 6:15am. They filed into winter coats, hats, mittens and boots and we began the drive downtown where thousands were gathering for the annual River Bank Run.

This year, two rookies were joining the masses. During the previous six weeks, my oldest daughter and I had been training together for this race. She had just turned eight years old.

Eight years old. Past the "cute and little" stage, but not quite yet to "snazzy and fashionable." A formidable age indeed. One that would require the creative attention of a mom. What does an eight year old need from her mom?

Well, I knew. She needed a 5K run. And she needed one with me, her mother.

The eight-year-old teeters on the verge of falling into the chasm of life's most treacherous stage – adolescence. Just reading that word sends shivers of memories through the spine of most parents. So I wanted to do something big to show my daughter that as she (okay, mostly I) anticipates this next stage, we would be able to experience the pain and triumph of life together.

For weeks we strapped on our running shoes and ran miles through our neighborhood. Each time we trained, we added a little more distance. Each time we trained, she assured me the extra distance would be impossible. Each time we trained, she was able to run the extra distance.

But here's the best part about our training: we held hands the entire time. Every step, every lunge, every struggle was experienced intimately, side-by-side, clutching each other's hand. The grip of "we can do this, but only if we stay together."

And that is what I wanted. See, this whole race idea was about one moment for me. That moment of crossing the finish line – together. That moment when I would look into my daughter's eyes and zoom in with the most profound mothering moment imaginable. I would capture her gaze and communicate with all of my gusto, "See? No matter how scared and tired and discouraged you get, you and I will be able to do hard things if we stick together. Stay by my side, baby girl, and we'll go places. I will be with you in the difficult, taxing moments. I am not going to stop supporting you and searching for that gleam in your eyes. My cheers will be near your ears."

I couldn't wait. It was going to be big. It would be the moment that would propel us into a successful future as mother and daughter. I was full of hope.

So after laughing at the weather, we began the race surrounded by thousands of runners and spectators. The only time we stopped running was to walk up a hill. We were holding hands the entire time. We turned the final corner. The fierce wind caused the purple and green finish line banner to flap wildly – waving us into its realm.

It was here. That moment I imagined. Savor each step, I thought. Squeeze her now sweaty palm. Get ready to unleash the award winning speech. Turn toward her glistening, blue eyes and....

She lets go.

Lets go!

She drops my hand. Drops my hand and starts sprinting on without me. She sprints and crosses the finish line – by herself. She doesn't want to finish with me. She wants to finish alone, and in front of me.

So much for seeing the glimmer in her eye. I only see the back of her head.

So I panic. The moment I dreamed of has disappeared. How will she know I will be with her in hard times if we don't cross the finish line looking into each other's eyes, with me saying super profound things to her? That was the whole reason we did this stupid race!

And then a deeper dream began to emerge. One that gently said, "This is why you are a parent. You're a mother so you can build strong foundations of confidence that only come from challenge and risk. You're a mother so you can have remarkable beginnings with your children. You're a mother so you can send your voice forward into the ears of your children. You're a mother so you can rejoice at the sight of the back of your child's head. You're a mother with hopes of being written out of the story of your children's lives so they can leave your story and tell their own, better, stronger, different story. To be a mom is to be at the starting line, but not the finish line."

TAKING NOTES

When this 'Study' season of mothering begins, you are holding your five-year-old daughter's hand, walking side by side with her. When it ends, your ten-year-old will have an emerging confidence and an identity that is separate from you.

Think back to the five-year-old. While she will certainly have increasing levels of independence, she will still need your help with many of her daily activities. She may know how to brush her hair, but you may be the one who puts in the French braids. She may enjoy painting her nails, but you will keep the activity confined to one location and cover the surface with layers of protective cloth. She may be able to select her outfits each day, but getting her snow boots off will still be a little tough. She may be learning how to read, but she will still need you to read to her. The beginning of this stage is wonderful. You can enjoy her steady growth, but her dependence on you remains steadfast.

These are days to savor.

The most significant way to help your daughter is to learn how to study her. At this stage, the makeup of her unique personality will be evident. Your understanding of her will help you guide her as you anticipate the challenges she will need to face in order to mature.

Become a student of your daughter. Her full-fledged personality will be shining in the moments that fill her days. Watch the way she expresses care (or lack of) for her bedroom. Listen to the conversations she has with her baby dolls. When she colors, does she do so silently or does she talk non-stop about everything that crosses her mind? Does she move through projects quickly or slowly? Is she quick to offer ideas and new directions or does she like her days to remain similar and consistent? Notice if she wears the same three outfits over and over again or if she changes her clothes five times a day.

Take note of all these details. The generative power of a mother comes when she can effectively interact with the unique wiring of her daughter.

If your daughter craves loud colors and gets excited by spontaneity, trying to impose a rigid schedule while dressing her in black and grey every day will drain her. If she refuels by pulling away in silence and you want to have lengthy conversations with her when she steps off the kindergarten bus, she will tire of you. If she lights up when she finds spider webs coated in dew and can identify bird calls at a young age, but you prefer to stay indoors, you will miss out on connecting with her during some of her most meaningful moments.

This study-project is crucial. By the end of this stage, your daughter will be passing you on the road, wanting to chart her own course. But she will still need your watchful eye and your discerning guidance so she can flourish and develop into the unique woman she was created to be.

EGYPTIAN STUDIES

My youngest is a hoot (can't that be said of all youngest children?). At age four, she, along with my older three children and several others, was asked to perform in a children's program at our church. One of the songs was, "Walk Like an Egyptian" by The Bangles. My kids each dressed up as ancient Egyptians with white, shimmery gowns, gold swaths and gold beaded headdresses. They had to do the Egyptian hand dance around their face while they crossed the stage and took their places among the rest of the crowd. This had been rehearsed 32,000 times. Finally, they were ready to do a performance for our church congregation.

At the end of the routine, the spot reserved for my youngest to stand was mistakenly taken by someone else. As the song finished, she sobbed hysterically, walking across the stage only to fall off of it into my arms, screaming at the top her lungs in front of countless people, "I WILL NEVER GO BACK TO THIS CHURCH AGAIN!"

What could I take away from that pleasant experience? My daughter did not come with skills that would naturally allow her to think of alternative options (for example, when someone is standing in the place you are to stand, find a different place to stand). Also, when there was an unexpected change that made her look like she had failed, she would feel deathly embarrassed

– which might result in her screaming super crazy things at the top of her lungs.

This was good for me to know about her. It helped me understand that, over the course of the next few years, I needed to place her in situations where she could have more of these experiences - in hopes that by the time she was grown, she would be able to respond differently.

Fast-forward two years. Same church. Smaller stage. Mostly kids in the audience. She was selected from the audience to play a game where she had to race another child and pick up trash on the stage. She was terrified. Absolutely terrified. I was by her side and told her this was something I wanted her to do. She took a deep breath and quietly asked, "Mom, when I come off the stage do you think you could just hold me for a minute?"

I've been here before.

Start at the finish line holding hands. End up staring at the back of the head.

This was my daughter's progression through this season. She began as someone without any coping skills when she felt threatened on stage. Now she was able to handle the fear, but was clearly still in need of maternal support and care.

My role in these two events was crucial. Knowing my daughter and her tendencies, quirks, pitfalls and strengths helped me to understand what was going on in her body. Along with this understanding, we needed a strong bond of trust between us. This is what we work so hard to create during the 'Generate' season.

When you use the beginning years to securely attach with your daughter, you can reap the benefits of that attachment by using your knowledge of her to provide the guidance she needs.

EXTREME MAKEOVER – DAUGHTER STYLE

Another daughter, when she was five years old, would hear my husband and I talk (only talk) about the possibility of remodeling our home years down the road. Whenever she would hear us, she would tear up and beg us not to change a thing in our house. She was certain that if we changed the house, she would feel like she had been kidnapped and wouldn't know where she belonged.

This is the same girl for whom I have cut larger armholes in her favorite nightgowns so she can continue to sleep in them for the fifth year in a row. She dreads getting her hair cut and would wear the same outfit every day if I allowed it. I did not have to study her for very long before I knew she does not enjoy change. In fact, change can bring about significant levels of anxiety in her. While there are fabulous strengths in loving life's consistencies, fearing change can be crippling.

So before we actually drove to a kitchen remodel store years later, I spent tremendous energy on this topic with her. We discussed her feelings repeatedly as I strategically placed her in situations that brought about exposure to healthy amounts of change. This was not easy. It took time and a lot of energy to help equip her with tools to handle this uncomfortable aspect of life.

Start at the finish line holding hands. End up staring at the back of the head.

What happened on that first trip to the kitchen remodel store? As we left, she told me she actually enjoyed it. And now that our house is redone, she giggles to think of how scared she was at the onset of the planning.

While we were able to successfully manage our way through the fear of the home remodel project, this will be a dynamic my daughter has to wade through her entire life. When she experiences something new and it appears threatening, she will most likely have to invest energy to arrive at a place of acceptance and comfort. This may never come naturally to her. My goal is to help her learn, as a young girl, the beginning steps to cope successfully with the challenge these events bring about in her life.

THAT'S INTERESTING!

So, what difficulties will we encounter during this stage? Two things.

First, there may be days when studying your daughter doesn't seem as interesting as studying Pinterest. Uploading those super cute photos of your daughter on Facebook may feel more urgent than focusing on her in real life. The thrill of finding sweet deals on Amazon may have more of a buzz than the contemplative curiosity of motherhood. In other words, this studious habit may feel boring.

Boring. When was the last time you felt bored? May I be so bold as to guess I may even need to write a definition of the word, due to its antiquated experience? Do you even remember what it feels like to be bored? I don't. I can't remember the last time I either had nothing to do or could not think of something to do, to the degree that it brought about a level of misery to my day.

I would venture to say that we have been conditioned to avoid being bored like we avoid admitting to another parent that our kid has never scored a goal during a soccer game. Boredom feels shameful to the active, involved and talented mom. We fear it will bring about the "you must be doing some major damage to your family" critique. The productive, busy mom is the good mom.

Elevating the skill of attentiveness will cause us to forfeit the flashy, plugged in, updated, just-checked-it-off-my-list glamour of today's mom. The process of getting to know your daughter will mostly be a quiet, contemplative experience that won't be lauded by impressed neighbors or confirmed with a complimentary email to your inbox. It could possibly be overlooked by everyone.

But here is the good news. As women, we have been uniquely gifted to perceive relational nuances. It may require more work for some of us than others, but you can be tuned in to non-verbal communication, subtle behaviors and the underlying stress that others feel. Our relational capacity enables us to take notice of particulars that make people interesting, sad, excited or motivated.

This studious aspect of motherhood may appear boring. In reality, it's a beautiful exercise of the generative nature of a woman - to look into the soul of another and know her. And when we live out our true calling and responsibilities, no 'pin' on Pinterest can match that thrill.

The second challenge in this task of studying your daughter is that it will never be complete. Never. You will never be able to say you are done noticing her, listening to the way she processes friendships, reflecting on her choices, marveling at her outfits and observing how she responds when she loses a game of Uno. In other words, the progress will feel slow at times. There may be light bulbs that go on in moments of, "I think I get her now!" But the next day you may forget what you learned or she may behave in a way that confuses your prior conclusion. She may, in fact, hold your hand during weeks of training and then let go of it during the last five seconds of a 5K race. Shocking, I know.

But this is truly the most beautiful, hopeful piece of this chapter – to be known.

I AM KNOWN

Do you know there is someone who watches you intimately? Who is full-eyed and eager to see what you did today? Was thrilled by the creative problem solving you used with the Barbie doll that lost its limb? Who was honored by the extra time you invested to make dinner nourishing for your family? Who listened as you encouraged your depressed neighbor? Who thought the color combination in your outfit was spot on? Who laughed when you told a funny story to your kids? And was amazed by the tenderness you showed when your little one fell and scraped her knee?

We are known. Deeply. Meaningfully. We are noticed and heard. Appreciated for the nuances that make our unique wirings special.

And when you know that is true, when you believe deep down that the Creator and Sustainer of the entire cosmos is absolutely fascinated with you, you can't help but want to give a taste of that to your little one.

GIVING OUR DAUGHTERS MORE – SEASON 2

1. Become a student of your daughter. Does she wear the same outfit four days in a row or does she change outfits four times a day?

2. Be your daughter's number one cheerleader as she progresses in growth through areas that pose great threat and stress.

3. Resist the temptation to think the viral life is more exciting than the intimate observation of your daughter.

Season 03: Guide

Age 10-13

Author: Katrina De Man

While Katrina knows she would have been best friends with Flannery O'Connor and her peahens on the farm in Georgia, she contents herself with the reality of her fine husband, five clever kids and plain 'ol chickens in Michigan. Hanging out with them is her best work, chickens mostly excluded. A long time ago, she used her English degree to administrate a group of radio guys and write a little copy but now she works to keep her kids learning, collecting favored authors and stories along the way. Coffee, good words and The Word bring intermittent moments of quiet to her soul.

MAKING MUSIC

School on Saturday? Not normal. But on this Saturday, hundreds of junior high kids wandered the halls, clothed in varied forms of black and white, waiting to perform. I was one of them. Dressed in black pants, white shirt, knee-high nylons and church shoes, my greatest struggle was to keep my anxious hands from rolling up my sheets of music. My instrument? It wasn't with me. No, I hadn't forgotten it. I just couldn't carry it. It was a piano.

I waited in the hallway, unsure of what would happen when I entered the classroom to perform. I knew there would be judges. And a piano, for sure. But a piano I'd never played before. I knew I'd be the focal point of everyone in the room. What I didn't know was how I would play. Would my performance be as good as my practice? I knew the music – perhaps too well. Now here I was. Waiting. Alone. Mind racing with what-ifs: What if, during those much-anticipated moments, I just couldn't translate the music from my eyeballs to my brain to my fingertips? What if my hands shook uncontrollably? What if I had to stop partway through? What if I cried? What if...

Then the door opened. The room monitor summoned me to enter. I was beyond ready and so relieved to finally perform that my what-ifs were already fading. I began by stating my name, my school and my hometown. The judges nodded and welcomed me to sit down on the piano bench. I arranged my music, made final adjustments to my positioning, double-checked my posture, took a deep breath and made music.

That was thirty years ago, but the scene and feelings are fresh. I easily recall the heaviness of my fear. My legs can't forget the feel of those black pants (I hated them). I felt ready, yet untried.

My experience from years ago makes me think of my own daughter. She's just around the corner from 11 years old. Just like me in my pre-adolescence, self-awareness, fear and risk-taking are waiting to greet her. She's beginning to think she might have something to offer. She's ready to start performing. Yet it's all new and untried. Therefore it's risky, frightening and possibly embarrassing. So what do I, as her mother, offer her?

Guidance.

I THINK I CAN

Do a quick survey of your geographical and social landscape – a mental walk through the neighborhood and school settings. Older girls, techy devices, maturing vocabularies, gender awareness, expanding social circles and secret collusions. It can leave any mother of daughters shivering with irrational fear.

As the light, delicate steps of childhood widen to those of a young girl at ages 10-13, a tipping point is reached. Complete dependence on parents morphs to a mid-independence as your daughter's self-talk changes from "maybe I can" to "I can." But this spreading of wings and the desire for independent experiences does not lessen your role as a mom. Rather, the mother-daughter partnership should grow and strengthen. Despite what she might express, your daughter is desperate for guidance. Guidance that involves all aspects of her person: mind, body and soul.

My pre-teen daughter needs me. She also needs teachers and coaches and church small-group leaders. For the most part, she's still okay with these needs. But I know the day will come soon when she tries to jettison her dependence and unashamedly announce that she's in control. And unlike my piano playing, life isn't a solo performance. At this stage of growing up it's meant to be a duet. Mom and daughter working together, sorting out categories of identity and passion and giftedness.

Keep studying your daughter. Notice whether she is making eye contact or just walking off without much of a wave. Does she move with confidence towards new experiences, or act shy and hesitant? Readiness and risk-taking garner new attentiveness.

Along the on-ramp to mid-independence are adult-like distractions that threaten to stunt (or accelerate) the path to healthy maturity. The pressures of growing up are timeless, but recent cultural forces have lured girls to adopt an aggressive image, complete with masculine traits. Today the blurring of gender is encouraged and expected. It's both subtle and overt. Your little girl, who not long ago was infatuated with dolls and dress-up, may soon drift toward toughness. She might spend her energy maintaining an abrasive edge of strength that hardens her to real emotion and healthy friendships. She might leverage her bent to manipulate for her own gain or seek dominance in relationships. Become a mean girl, or a bully. Or be bullied.

It all seems so scary. And fragile. So how do we guide our daughters through the minefield of growing up? How do we push back on culture while entering in? How do we mold and shape pliable minds in ways that are pure and noble and life-giving and truly feminine? How do we help our daughters understand the true beauty and wonder of their bodies?

By talking.

Often.

CAN WE TALK?

Communication with my daughters is non-negotiable. Dialogue is *life* to our relating. Frequent, positive interactions foster confidence – confidence my girls need to accept and embrace their femininity.

But in the talking, it's easy to blow it. As my girls have entered this pre-teen season, I've rehashed moments from our past that have gone poorly. Those times we talked *at*, but not really *to*, each other. In my looks back I've learned that if I'm not able to offer myself grace for conversational mistakes, I certainly won't find the humility required to forgive and work through these with my daughter.

My daughters and I have some additional communication complications. We deal with the typical two-ships-passing-in-the-night pre-adolescent posturing, but we've also inherited cultural distance. Both of my girls are adopted from a foreign country. So in addition to studying their faces and body language, I've had to step back and contextualize their interpretation of my words. When their eyes dart or their chins shoot out or their smile doesn't reach their eyes, I'm being offered immediate non-verbal feedback – the wires between us have crossed. Adopted or not, our daughters will project these signals, and it's critical for us to catch them.

Communication is key to all parent-child relationships. Still, there are times when talking isn't good. Like when I'm talking – a lot. I've come to know that I'm flubbing an opportunity when I'm talking, and my daughter isn't. When I'm barreling into the heart of a five-paragraph diatribe and her big dark eyes transition from bright to glazed. In those moments, I feel the conscious prompt to stop but momentum works against me. I blow through the stop signs of motherly instinct like a car on an icy road. That's when I must work hard to pause. Take a breath. Create some space with a bit of silence and plead, "Help me, Jesus. Spirit, come. Give me Your wisdom."

I HAVE A QUESTION...

My pleas get answered. Sometimes in the moment, sometimes later. And the wisdom received often leads me to craft questions. Questions aimed at drawing my daughter out. Questions that take us both back to that juncture when one of us took a wrong turn. Simple, but direct questions. Open-ended questions like,

"What did you like about the movie last night?" instead of "Did you like the movie?" Or, "What do you think would have been a better choice in that situation?" Open-ended questions are less threatening and communicate my readiness to listen.

Of course, I also have to reject the conversation killers. Those questions that usually spring from my knee-jerk reactions. You've heard them. Probably spoken them. And likely had them spoken to you. Questions that begin like this: "Why did you…?" or "Haven't I said…" or "How many times…" or "Why can't you…" There's no life in those questions. No open door to dialogue. No chance to know or be known. No guidance. And when I really get rolling toward that nagging mom place, I might employ the bad tact of speculating about my daughter's thoughts and motivations rather than letting her speak for herself. It can sound like this: "When you did that, I bet you were thinking…" or "You just did that because…" Such things lead to more misunderstanding and extinguish any opportunity of productive communication, removing a chance to know more of what's happening in my daughter's heart and mind.

These closed-ended questions and other poor parenting moments can result in fitful nights of sleep. I really dislike messing up. I can get pretty down on myself knowing that I should have just taken time with my daughter in the moment. Bit my tongue (for real) and asked her to remind me again of what she was saying.

Sometimes, often after the fact, I startle myself with realization about a conversation gone badly. I'll think, "Oh, no! That wasn't *her* point, it was *mine*!" as I trace my harsh response back to a story I read in *People Magazine* while at the orthodontist. Which I then projected onto my daughter. Which then fostered a fear that if I don't nip 'this' it will bloom into 'that' and then "people" will know that I was a negligent mom whose girl has gone wild and is now making headlines.

Ugh!

How easy it is for me to be driven by idealized fear and worry. Bringing this anxiety into conversations with my daughter results in pulling out the young and tender shoot of her life and tossing it onto the compost pile like a weed. My fear can move me to quick judgment of my daughter rather than to God-given peace and wisdom that will help me pursue her through open-ended questions. Perhaps she's just innocently curious and wants my input and encouragement. Perhaps she's not looking to make her own "Girls Gone Wild" video. I must always keep in mind: give grace first, then truth. I have to be quick with forgiveness – for her, and me – because the mistakes will surely come.

Mistakes and all, I seize even the briefest one-on-one moments to chat. I also schedule time together so normal conversation can occur (i.e. she talks, I listen, then we dialogue). As we dialogue, I'm intentional with how I guide her through conflict. I ask her how she feels. I enter her struggles as I share age-appropriate examples of my own struggle with the urge to be in control and manipulate. Talking to each other — in good and not-so-good moments — is a lifeline we hold with our tightest grip.

We all know that talking is essential when it comes to the rite of passage into womanhood. It's a wonderful and terrible part of being a female. A periodic reminder of our role as life-giver. But at times that 'life' can feel like death. You know what I'm talking about.

Your period.

CH-CH-CH-CHANGES

In this stage of development, your daughter sits on the brink, or has already been sucked into menstrual mayhem. Oh, the horror of hormones! Crabbiness, insecurity, emotional warfare and irrational behavior. How easy it is to blame our attitudes and actions on our cycle. Use it as a convenient scapegoat. For sure, the physiological effects of our monthly visitor are unavoidable. But our response to it is not. As our daughters get whisked into the girl-to-woman metamorphosis, time with a mom who relates with patience and understanding can yield strong footholds of influence. So guide your girl with positive perspective on her blossoming, life-giving abilities. Talk in good times and grumpy times. It will help settle the craziness of change.

To spice things up (as if more excitement is needed once 'the cycle' starts cycling), cue the boys. And the confusion. Those cute little boys your daughter played with for years in innocence suddenly find their way to her heart. Overnight, who's getting whose attention becomes important. Way too important. Old securities dance away as early adolescence barges in without knocking. It's all quite overwhelming. For you, and her. What to do?

Talk.

And what about loaded topics like body weight, clothing, or homosexuality? These issues may stir storminess in your relating. Welcome them. Enter dialogue with your daughter without hesitation or shame. Our kids need information. They need their thought processes checked and carefully mentored. They need motherly guidance. We can't let a jury of peers at a junior high lunch table decide our daughter's ideal weight, style of dress or social acceptability.

HAIR WARS

Even though I want to protect my little girl from the cruelty that can come from peers, there are times I can be just as hurtful.

Like the time I said to her, "No way! Everyone agrees you're too young for chemicals in your hair." Seriously. The upkeep and time required with a straightening iron literally gives me the shakes. I want our Ethiopian beauty to keep it au naturel. Chris Rock and I? Totally on the same page with Afro hair. But my daughter and me, we've walked around the 'different hair' block a dozen times. My persuasive speech refuting irrational hairdos is always at the ready. Because, moms, this is one of those 'special' situations, right? A situation when our little girls aren't thinking clearly and we need to set them straight. In such times we're entitled to ditch the principle of asking good questions and head straight to "I talk, you listen."

And that's what I did. I even dosed out a measure of spirituality to keep my argument tight. After all, I only want my lovely, dark-skinned daughter to accept her image-bearing reality. Every morning as she combs through her not-so-coarse but thick and curly hair she should be savoring what many others envy. I don't want her to live in the dark place of I'm-not-good-enough-as-God-created-me. From my perspective, my motives were very noble.

But during the last battle in the war of hair, my daughter's face – brave yet vulnerable with knowing disappointment – brought me a new revelation. It's her hair, and she's tired of it. And what girl isn't drawn to the sleek hair movements on those Pantene commercials? How could I forget that every female loves choice and variety? With first-time clarity, I saw my fear as the real reason for our hair wars. Fear that she'd take a "yes" and develop into a discontented adult female looking for love in all the wrong places. Fear that if I allow this, something terrible will follow (remember my *People Magazine* mistake?). I realized that I was assigning motives to my daughter that might not exist. I was projecting expectations onto her. What she needed (and needs) is my love. My ongoing affirmation of her beauty – no matter how she styles her hair. She needs my peaceful, patient guidance through the barrage of cultural messages that beg her to conform to an unachievable, airbrushed image.

I want my daughter's heart to be wholly devoted to her Father and Creator. I'm not sure I want to sacrifice that goal on the altar of hair. Helping her enjoy a neutral desire can bring a deeper level of trust and joy to our relationship. Initially I thought *my* heart was for her in my "no." But what I missed was *her* heart. I didn't have it because I wasn't listening. Our trips around the 'different hair' block could have been halved if I had listened and asked open-ended questions. Instead, my hardness bound her with my fear and anxiety. A common mom mistake. I'm super glad I stopped talking at her and started listening to her. That's a win for my daughter – and for me.

MIND GAMES

When I talk but don't listen, I teeter on the edge of generating shame in my little girl. Shame is everywhere. It leeches into good places like a toxin. Like water behind an over-burdened dam, it pushes its victims toward pain and confusion as it lingers and divides. Shame can undermine our best relational moments with insidious precision. It has a lethal ability to imprison us with negative self-talk. Thankfully, there's freedom from shame – both when we're shamed, and when we do the shaming. That freedom comes when we discover the seeds from which shame sprouts.

Exploring seeds of shame with your tween girl can bring tremendous yield. As you gently blow back shame's smoke screen, light will shine on deeper issues. You'll help her recognize that shame is often a string of lies whispered alongside truth. Appropriately sharing about your own experiences can bring safety to prickly topics like shame.

How could 'hair wars' have played out in a more productive, shameless way? Here's an example:

My daughter: *Mom? I wish I could have straight hair…*

Me: *What? No way. I never heard you say that before! (said tongue in cheek)*

My daughter: *(Sheepish smile. Worried eyes.)*

Me: *Talk to me about straight hair. What does it mean to you?*

My daughter: *It doesn't mean anything to me. It just seems easier.*

Me: *Is this just about easy? Or could it be that you want to try straight for a while because all your friends have straight hair?*

My daughter: *(mild snicker, but continuing eye contact, no words though, lots of thinking.)*

Me: *You DO have good hair, mainly because it's what God created you with. BUT…I do recognize the girl inside you peeking out and I am beginning to realize how important this is for you. You just want to give straight hair a try.*

My daughter: *Yes. (nodding, bobbing and all sorts of general, non-verbal, hopeful agreement.)*

Me: *Well…this is a stretch for me, but I'm gonna say yes to curly – I mean straight hair!*

My daughter: *(enthusiastic hugs and general declarations of my amazing mom status)*

As you talk about shame in good ways with your daughter, speak your thoughts out loud. Doing so disarms shame's power. And once disarmed, those seeds can be rooted out. At times, shame points to convictions, which are good to uphold with balance. But other times shameful feelings highlight issues that need love and guidance. Whatever the case, work hard to confront the shadow shame often casts upon women. Speak directly. Deal with shame like the big, nasty spider it is. Crush it and leave it behind.

Along with shame are two more ruling desires that plot to control our minds: envy and comparison. The pull is strong for women to see themselves through the eyes of others. The opinions of peers and boys gain traction for a girl at this tween stage. In his book, *Girls on the Edge*, Dr. Leonard Sax suggests, "Girls who are dressing in hot pants prior to the onset of puberty are not expressing their sexuality. They don't have, and should not have, a sexual agenda to express. Dressing sexually in the absence of sexual desire is simply conformism."[4] Schooling choice and media restrictions are not perfect insulators from the desire to fit in. To be accepted. The attacks on self-image often come from within.

So guide and protect your daughter with regular conversation about envy and comparison. Here are a few things to consider as these games of the mind ramp up:

- Comparison and envy are freedom killers.
- Comparison is similar to shame. It keeps us from being

enabled and engaged.

- Comparison can divide relationships in two forms. One is about superiority: I am so much better. The other is about defeat: I could never do that.
- Envy displaces the ability to genuinely serve and give to others.
- Theodore Roosevelt said that comparison is "the thief of joy." Envy and comparison rob the feminine heart of contentment and joy.

Give your daughter a leg-up on the emotions and concerns that can confuse, befuddle and complicate. She needs your help deciphering the self-talk that circulates in her developing mind. Talk that makes her question her beauty and worth. Talk that can warp a healthy self esteem. Consistent dialogue about themes of shame, envy and comparison will help your daughter become an emotionally mature woman.

READ THIS?

The female mind is a wonderfully mysterious thing. It's crafted for relationship and engagement. It's created to emote and process and produce. It's the data center for life-giving. So when it comes to our daughters, we must not neglect the privilege of developing their beautiful minds.

I grew up in a small town. It had a bank, two corner bars, a bowling alley, a knife factory and a paper mill. It also had a library. I could walk out my door, scoot through my neighbors' backyards, walk a block up the street past the fire department (which was right across the road from the very creepy, for sure haunted-even-in-the-daytime house), up a little hill, turn the corner, go half a block more, then cross the street to the library. Seven minutes one way. I walked this route often because I loved to read. I started with beloved storybooks like, *Caps for Sale* and *Charlotte's Web* and *Ramona Quimby*. But from there, I was clueless as to where my maturing reading abilities and tastes should take me.

As I picked out books on my own, some were thick with words and slowly developed characters. Others had bigger font and were more entertaining. Over time, I gravitated to the entertaining books because, really, who doesn't want to read about gorgeous blond girls – cheerleaders and really smart – who have great clothes and the best boys in school vying for their affections? Those *Sweet Valley High* twins had it all – even when they were bickering. These stories were my un-reality and the food with which I fed my mind. Worldview in 200 pages, and I devoured every last bit of it. My feminine soul was hungry for definitions of femininity. These books were eager to meet my need.

Not long after I left the college scene in the early 1990s, it came to the attention of many – parents, teachers, publishing houses – that kids were too sophisticated for the teen books of that day. Just like today's kindergarteners meet the first grade skill requirements of children from previous decades, kids were consuming life at a younger age – or at least wanted to. Relevance is everything, right? Parents observed their children ditching youth fiction for stories of adult horror and romance novels. This plunged young adults into mature themes of violence, intricate drama and detailed sex. The response from publishers was a new genre of books. A genre packed with intensity, peril and independence. Stories that mock traditional values, glamorize sexual freedom and blur gender distinctions. A new reality emerged as children began living in the same social and relational world as adults.

THE POWER OF IMAGINATION

Movies, TV and books (take your pick) wield the power to control a young girl's thought life. Her vivid imagination, so fragile and in need of careful development and shaping, can be overloaded and grown up too fast. Technology provides the vehicle that can transport each of us into unsafe, unhealthy destinations. That veil which protected the delicate growth of our imagination is gone. Our culture provides a vast buffet on which to gorge: the colors, the action, the clothes, the houses, the cars. The food doesn't smell, but the storyline is a complete kit, ready at the click of a button.

Young girls will crave adult storylines. Our daughters yearn to know, "What is love? What is sex? What if I don't have either? Am I beautiful?" As Dr. Leonard Sax states in his book, *Girls on the Edge*, "girls today are bombarded with the notion that revealing your body is a valid means of self-expression, even a manifestation of 'girl power.' As parents, we must reject the notion that girls have to reveal their bodies in order to empower themselves."[5] Left unguarded and unguided, your daughter will have her head stuffed full of unfiltered, damaging answers. Society offers heroines that are strong and independent with male sidekicks that are gorgeous, inept and all-too-willing to let her lead. The feminist movement baits women on achievement, clout and the power to arrange their world. The man-child will follow along behind us (or so we're told), content to settle into a happy state of extended adolescence.

But how has that worked for us, ladies? Beware the cultural story that plays to a girl's already well-honed ability to arrange (said another way, manipulate). Beware that which further assists a man with passivity and risk avoidance. For women, the storylines of independence, perfect romance, Fourth-of-July sexual experiences and man-crushing strength are just as addicting as heroin. The danger of these worldviews is real. They stimulate hormones that create a craving for more of the same. Romance novels feed those addictive hormones. So does porn – emotional porn as well as visible porn. Today's teen girls have the ability to arm themselves with a technological arsenal that allows them to bypass traditional options and satisfy their cravings. Time runs through our fingers as young girls pop status updates, text messages, books, magazines and movies like Tic-Tacs, aggravating a hunger that gets kicked further down the road.

So help your daughter. Be intentional with shaping her moral imagination. A young girl needs to read plenty of good, old-fashioned fairy and classic tales. This isn't just stodgy, moldy writing. There are many choices from years past. And with discernment, you'll find modern writers that are putting out great material too. Find stories about situations that have choices and paths and often cost the characters something valuable. Through story, you'll gift your daughter with a pattern for developing her mind. She'll awaken to what can come from the confident choices (good and bad) modeled in these tales. Start simple and small. Find a highly recommended story with classic forms* and read it together at least once a week. Or read the book and then watch the movie. And in the reading and watching, talk. (Note: a list of recommended book appears at the end of this chapter.)

Along with reading, keep your daughter's hands busy. Meaningful work will broaden her development and expand her mind. Young girls need tasks that contribute in a regular way to the household. Even if your daughter is busy with school and sports, small jobs like sweeping floors, doing dishes, or folding laundry keep her connected to family responsibilities. It's a 'must have' arena for her to live in. The needs of managing a home don't go away. Help her grasp the life-giving value she brings through responsible household contributions. It will prepare her for later, when marriage, family or professional pursuits get added in.

WHAT'S YOUR STATUS?

Social networking is a natural outlet for conversation about clothes and boys and other girls and the imagination. Emails, messages, texts, blogs, tweets and feeds. During this 'Guide' season, your girl has likely spied the technology buffet and wants to taste. Guidance by mom and constant dialogue must be part of her diet.

Walking through that maze with my girls requires me to regulate my own appetite for media. I knew that Facebook had an unhealthy hold on me the day I realized I was taking mental note of every fun, unique, enjoyable, witty moment with my kids and crafting it into a status update. It was a wake-up call. I joined Facebook with strong reservations. I really didn't need something else to maintain. Email was enough. But I'd been hearing how great Facebook was for keeping in touch with family and long-distance friends. Sounds great. I'm in!

I quickly stumbled upon some friends from college. I totally loved being in touch with them again. I thought, "This is great! Facebook *is* a good thing!" But then some other "friends" found me. You know what I'm talking about. Then the parade of private messages revved up. I was soon sucked into relational problems with people I didn't even know. I felt the stress of caring about events and hurts that were way outside my circle of influence. Several times a day I was yanked into emotional entanglements. All the while, I had six sets of non-virtual eyeballs staring at mine – that is, when mine weren't mesmerized by the blue and white of the Facebook screen.

I began to resent the interruptions and banal posts. Still, part of me was enticed by the endless banter. I could easily justify my Facebook time with those good re-connections with family and old friends. But it was a major tug of war. My life was fracturing. I couldn't balance my virtual relationships with the time and energy needed by those sitting just a few feet away from me and my computer. Facebook was sucking me dry.

As my daughter inches closer to her entrance upon the social networking scene, I can't stop studying her. I must know her pulls and potential weaknesses when it comes to the virtual realm. Online living should never usurp our living, breathing life. It's not difficult to buy the lie that attention online means identity and purpose. To replace quiet moments at home with online busyness is to misunderstand the richness of having time to be lonely and aimless. Such times of void can drive us to better self-understanding. And God. Self-reflection is invaluable. Solitude is vital. As a mom, I can use my own tensions and struggles and successes to help my daughter make good decisions with her online presence.

So, what's my current status with Facebook? I've pulled out – for a time. When I realized my struggle, I knew I needed space to assess and regenerate my focus. This came at a time when school was starting, the holidays were approaching fast, and the best use of my energy was to step back. There will be another time when I reactivate that account, reengage with college friends, and know the ins and outs of my nieces' social life. I look forward to that. Maybe by then, my daughter will be posting status updates alongside me and together we'll ride the tension.

Virtual connectedness is not going away. As moms, we must be active and involved – even if we aren't there ourselves. If you're there already with your daughter, you know what those first few days feel like as she sets up shop and starts posting statuses. It doesn't take long to get a glimpse into her heart, her insecurities, her self-indulgences and her level of respect. It may be your best litmus and your worst nightmare. It may be her worst nightmare, too. Virtual constructs give the false security that we are connected and in control and that relationship is about quick words and short phrases. But vast impressionistic kingdoms, built on titillating photos, status updates and varying responses from the crowd, rise and fall overnight.

And so we find that this season of guiding and shaping is not just about skill awareness. It's also about imagination awareness. Females live in their imaginations. Made for relationships, it's easy to craft a story in our minds in 12 seconds and then relive that story a dozen different ways over the next 45 minutes. A girl sees a cute boy and soon, in her mind, they rendezvous at Starbucks, share a Salted Caramel Frappuccino, and talk. He reaches across the table to hold her hand. So simple, yet so alive! Her mind races to their leaving. She imagines her sweater has slid off her shoulder, her skin exposed to the cold air. He notices, and gently lifts it back into place, grazing her skin with his touch. They'll share a look. She's no longer feeling cold.

A woman's mind needs little coaxing to be swept away with provocative nicely-packaged imaginings. We are driven by deeply hoped-for stories – stories that come from our hearts, beliefs and goals. We crave romance because we were created for man, and from man. But our sinful nature has twisted that good desire. We love the excitement of being pursued. Of being told we're beautiful. Those desires and longings point to our need to love and be loved purely and completely by our

Heavenly Father.

Our responsibility as a mother – and extreme privilege – involves nurturing healthy desire while developing the mind. Our own mind, as well as our daughter's. We need a diet that fosters a virtuous imagination and healthy cravings and real relationships. Relationships not frantic with doing, but knowing and being known. Redemptive relationships that draw us deeper into God's story. For it's only in that story that we'll find security, significance, and beauty in the truest love of all.

BALANCING ACT

Walking alongside your daughter as her mind and body start to blossom is both exciting and exhausting. Before you can help your daughter find joy in competence and accomplishment, you need to understand yourself. What brings you joy? How do you find rest? Your to-do list has grown beyond "keep them alive" but the pull to be on top of it all remains. Balance pursuits, passions and responsibilities so you can bring order and ease to your life and the life of your family. Do the daily work of shifting affections to what is truly satisfying – a deep faith and trust in God. Only He gives us value and qualifies our worth. He empowers us toward a life that cultivates the attributes of the Spirit – love, joy, peace, patience, kindness, goodness and self-control. Rest arrives when you say, "I'll obey and trust You, Lord Jesus."

A woman's settled heart is a beautiful gift to everyone she encounters. When mom is at rest, the family finds its pace. Life involves task and pleasure. Grocery shopping, cooking and baking, laundry, housecleaning, professional pursuits, exercise – the list is our bane. We want to believe balance doesn't matter. Yet, the more settled we are – the more we die to our misplaced desire – the more we'll be able to step in to guide our daughters, bless our families, and be women who reflect the glory of our Creator.

As your daughter tips from "maybe I can" to "I can", work hard to seize opportunities that generate balance for her, too. Lead her into rest after a job well done. Notice when she brings a good attitude to a mundane task. Acknowledge when she talks with you instead of burying or pushing away her hurt. Highlight and celebrate these special moments with her. Those moments are like a flower just after dawn – fresh, maybe dewy – its strong petals opening with soft movements that are full of tomorrow. There will be harsh winds and heavy showers. There will always be pruning shears. Nurture the soil of your daughter's life with wisdom and direction. Generate life for her from your own life. Then watch closely for the blossoms of dawn.

MOM WAS RIGHT

Now, back to where this all began: memories of a music competition.

Thing is, I never thought about taking piano lessons. It wasn't something I begged to do. But my mom had been studying me. She observed I was quick with music. I could hear it and flow naturally with it. I could sing. I was comfortable expressing through song in public settings. Something in my mom's gut said, "get this girl some piano lessons." So when I was in sixth grade, mom and I made a habit of trekking together in our green Chevy station wagon to Mrs. Hess' house. Three dollars for a half-hour of piano lessons.

My mom was right. She knew me and guided me toward

something that brought me joy. Gave me confidence. Developed my mind. Helped me rest. I couldn't have done it without her.

And now my daughter can't do it without me.

GIVING OUR DAUGHTERS MORE – SEASON 3

1. Recreating together: craft, exercise, cook, bake together.

2. Read a book together, then watch the movie (if applicable).

3. Ask follow-up questions – hours, days, or weeks later – after difficult times and conversations.

4. Continue to study your girl and her awakening interests and tastes.

More classic books to consider:

The Phantom Tollbooth by Norton Juster
Dr. Jekyll and Mr. Hyde by Robert Louis Stevenson
The Velveteen Rabbit by Margery Williams
The Princess Bride by William Goldman
The Cay by Theodore Taylor
The Book of the Dun Cow by Walter Wangerin, Jr.
Anne of Green Gables by L.M. Montgomery
Jane Eyre by Emily Bronte
Sense and Sensibility by Jane Austen
Little Women by Louisa May Alcott
A Wrinkle in Time by Madeleine L'engle
The Giver by Lois Lowry
The '*Shoe*' books by Noel Streatfeild

Newer books that have classic potential:

Lizzie Bright and the Buckminster Boy by Gary Schmidt
Wild Wednesdays by Gary Schmidt
The Mistmantle Chronicles by M.I. McAllister
The Wingfeather Saga by Andrew Peterson

The Ashtown Burials by ND Wilson
The *100 Cupboard* series by ND Wilson
The *Tillerman Cycle* series by Cynthia Voigt

*Classic literature has these elements: a story with a moral lesson that is decades old. The story is returned to time and again across generations and demographics. The author is famous. Though the story is appealing and accessible, it is difficult to read and is often lengthy. The story has spin-offs or copy cat novels based on its premise. Supremely popular in the time period written.

Season 04: Engage

Age 13-18

Author: Lori Cook

Lori is committed to Ron, her husband of 26 years, and her two daughters. Lori studied at Cambridge University in England and graduated from Hope College. She has been in the media for 28 years, serving as an advocate for children and families on television, radio, print and on-line. She is passionate about her family, her community, her work and her mission.

TEXT ME IF YOU LIKE ME

She's been in there for over an hour. The door is shut. I hear nothing. My mom-sense is peaked at code red. I'm tense. Something's going down. My intuition says a boy is involved.

Slowly, the bedroom door creeks open and my teenage daughter emerges, a tear sliding down her face. She quickly wipes it away, hoping I didn't notice. Without making eye contact she mutters a pitiful, "everything's fine." We both know it's not.

I move closer to stand beside her. I reach out and gently squeeze her hand. I risk moving in with a gentle, softly spoken question. Then another. I offer my lightest, loving engagement. After a few moments of brief but healing exchanges, she raises her hand that clutches an over-used tissue and her cell phone. With wavering voice, she reads me a text message. From a boy. Just as I thought. And like most guys his age, he's a light-year (or two) behind girls relationally. His typed-out words are sharp. Lasting. Void of non-verbal context. And they sting, perhaps even more than spoken words.

This is social life for teens today. Some date, most do not. It's a technological landscape that we – the parents, the experienced ones – never traveled. Some things haven't changed. Guys still ask girls for their phone numbers. Not to call, but to text them. Getting to know someone no longer involves face-to-face conversation, but 'conversation' via 140 character volleys that often string into the wee hours of the night. Gone are the days of face-to-face. Asking someone out usually isn't a heart pounding experience. Just IM them. It's less risky – literally, and virtually.

This form of 'dating' and break-up may surprise us as moms. But it doesn't surprise our children. It's how things work in their circles. Messaging isn't just convenient, it's life. And whether we like it or not, this reality brings us to a scary place. We must accept that the rules have changed and we can't parent from our own youthful experiences.

When I was a teen, if my parents wondered what was going on in my life they simply followed the phone cord. It often led to a closet, which was locked. I was inside, chatting like crazy. If they wanted, they could position themselves on the other side of the door and listen. They could glean a muffled window into my life through the laughter and frustration and surprise of my phone conversations. If that didn't suffice, or if there was greater urgency to obtain key information, mom could conveniently arrange a special delivery of folded laundry to my room. It was no secret that my diary lay open on my nightstand. A bit of innocent browsing offered her glimpses of my soul.

Today, diaries seem as rare as a flip phone. Few girls use them, and some that do aren't really writing to themselves in meaningful ways. Facebook, instant messaging and texting have sentenced diaries to a slow death on a Wal-Mart clearance shelf. The same is true for phone calls – they just don't happen. Gone are the days of waiting by the phone to make a call, or waiting for a certain someone to call you. There's no waiting, period. In fact, why do phone companies offer call waiting? Nowadays, if you call and get someone's voicemail, or the line happens to be busy, what do most do? Hang up and send a text (which begins with "I tried to call you but"). This is our modern relational exchange: silent, instant, prescribed, arranged.

OUT OF THE LOOP

It seems reasonable to keep pace with our daughter's text message conversations, right? After all, how much relating can she really do using that tiny keypad in short, abbreviated, cryptic bursts?

More than I thought.

This season of parenting gives little time for parents to recover from "intro to social networking." Without a break, we're forced headlong into multi-tasking mania. And many times, I can't keep up. My daughters can communicate with dozens of friends with handfuls of simultaneous texting groups. I've found my simple question of, "So, who are you texting?" to be naïve, and way too complicated. And I've learned to not even ask, "What are you guys talking about?" It's difficult to wander through the entanglement of six IM relationships all playing out at the same time. I'm trying to keep up, to be a student of my daughters, to listen and talk with them, but the frenetic pace and constant rule changes can leave me frazzled.

And the relational world of my girl can leave me feeling alone. Out of the loop. Left out. I'm often empty when it comes to knowing what's really going on. I'm tempted to grab her phone and read through the long strings of messages. Peruse the apps she's downloaded. Scroll through the tweets she sends. Scour the profiles of those she's following.

Truth is, even if I acted on that temptation, I can barely navigate through the menus on her smartphone. My daughter makes it looks so effortless. Much like my talking on the phone was when I was her age. So what's a mom to do?

Engage.

And pray – a lot.

It's easy to be overwhelmed. To feel inept with smartphones, status updates, tweets and texting lingo. The well-worn path of cynicism is tempting. Perhaps you've walked it, even for a bit. It's the path traveled by parents who disengage, and can be heard muttering, "kids these days." But walking that path brings death, not life. Walking that path means I refuse to be a mom who does the hard work of studying my daughter. What she loves. How she struggles. How I can guide and shape her passions and pursuits. It prevents me from entering her pain and crying with her.

NO OSTRICHES

So I need to keep learning and asking questions. Technology is not going away. Our daughters may abandon their Facebook or open a secret account. They might bail to a different venue, like Twitter, if they sense parents are crowding their social spaces. They may pop in and out of several communities just to stay distant from the drama. They will come and go and come again.

But one thing is sure – texting, tweeting, instant messaging and Facebooking are accepted communication tools in our society. As a mom, I can't play Ostrich by sticking my head in the sand. I must engage with grace and love and patience. I must work daily to be soft to the reality that even on those days when the house isn't big enough for both of us – she really needs me. She's looking to me, her life-giver, to guide her through boys and tech and fashion and purity into her own womanhood. I'm not allowed to throw my hands in the air because I just don't get it or wish things were different. Instead, I trust God when I feel helpless. Then I engage.

As I've moved into the lives of my teenage girls with intentionality, here are a few things I've learned in the tensions of life and tech:

- I need to encourage good choices with technology based on what I've instilled in them through the 'Study' and 'Guide' seasons of their growing-up. Technology is just another venue, bringing new opportunities to dialogue about our imaginations, self-image, and insecurities.
- I need to hold the same standards in the virtual world as I do in real life. I value respect for self and others. I want to have a kind spirit. I want to be truthful. These qualities should be true about me and my girls – both on and off-line.

- Who we are in the virtual world should mirror who we are in the real world. Too many of us create 'impressionistic kingdoms' that are disconnected from reality.
- Enforce the same consequences you would in the real world when boundaries are ignored in the virtual world. If your daughter is behaving badly on-line, handle it the same way you would if it were happening in your living room.
- I remind my daughters that I can, and do, check which numbers they engage with the most. It's a relentless, tiring task. But necessary.

ANOTHER DIET?

As women, we are all too familiar with dieting – in good, and not so good ways. A diet is one way to control and monitor intake. And control is helpful, not just with food, but also with things like media.

A healthy media diet is crucial for cultivating an environment where our children can thrive. Where they feel comfortable, confident, and secure. That means some tough choices. And boundaries. It requires limiting screen time and being, perhaps, the 'weird' parent. You know, the one all your daughter's friends talk about. But we've got to be okay with weirdness. The life and values we are striving to give our daughters are more important than being seen as relevant and permissive and easily taken advantage of. Just like we wouldn't allow our children to drink Monster and eat Doritos all day, we need to provide a balanced media diet. No doubt, the 'always on, always connected' reality of our culture can tempt us like chocolate cake. Yet our motherly role requires awareness and monitoring and guidance when it comes to the media diet of our children – and for us.

One thing that helped my daughters and me ease into our technological engagement was a limited data plan. That's right. Even though it's simpler and sometimes less expensive to go with unlimited or bundled everything, my recommendation is this: don't do it. I say that with grace, because I know how easy it is to make decisions looking primarily through the lens of family economics. Couple a tight budget with a slick Verizon rep and in a matter of minutes your firm hold on principle slips away as you sign a two-year contract.

So, thoughtfully consider a limited media plan. Yes, that will require more upfront work, and more management month-to-month. But restricting minutes will be a great help when it comes to establishing boundaries. It will also aid in monitoring media consumption and fostering appetites for things other than virtual engagement. But be warned. You will be surprised along the way. I sure was.

One of my daughters loves to text message. A little too much. Her entrance on the texting scene was fast and furious. Just a few months into the venture, I was shocked by the list of overages. Initially, I was most shocked at myself. I was keeping close track of our data consumption. How could this have happened? But I soon realized that it's nothing for a young adult to send and receive hundreds of text messages in a single day. That's several thousand in one month. How could I possibly stay on top of this? Help! Can I play Ostrich now?

Once things settled, those overages provided a good lesson for our entire family. My text-happy daughter did extra chores in exchange for her indulgence. She learned to think more carefully about the messages she sent. I learned a few things as well. No matter how much I try to control, my daughter still has the choice to join me – or not. And despite the choice she might make today, my call to be her mother doesn't change. So I pursue her in her happiness, and grumpiness. I'm actively involved in her life, whether it's technology or homework or drama group or soccer club or the creepy boy that just texted, "see ya!" I must dialogue, not IM her. As she moves through the seasons of maturation, I spend time learning her fears and insecurities. I walk beside her and guide her into her feelings and emotions. I help shape her thoughts of herself and the God who loves her.

IT TAKES A VILLAGE

All this talk of technology might seem over the top. But no matter your level of technological engagement, your daughter lives in a virtual world. So do her friends. As moms, we can struggle to gauge where our daughters are at relationally and emotionally. How do we keep the closeness we had in the early years?

In the season of 'Guide' we emphasized the need to talk with our daughters. It's even more critical in these years when texting and media try to silence our efforts to know our girls. As our teenager matures, the points of contact for conversation must broaden. As she gains independence, we'll need to brace ourselves for disappointment. It's possible, even likely, that she'll share some of her deepest longings and desires with someone else. We may lose our exclusivity, and we need to be okay with that. It's normal and healthy for our daughters to seek opinions and advice from others in this season.

Instead of sulking or retreating when your daughter looks to someone other than you, step into it. Engage. Help her to establish relationships with trusted women – young and old. These can be your friends, college girls at church, small-group leaders, employers, teachers…you get the point. Allow your daughter to build her own relationships with several godly women while she's in junior high. Then, as she progresses through her teen years it won't be odd when one of these older friends wants to meet your daughter for coffee, needs her help with a project, or invites her to join a Bible study.

This widened circle of influence can be a wonderful asset to your mothering. This 'village' of women can step into gaps that will naturally open in your relationship with your teen girl. Gaps that grow out of your daughter's healthy procession from girl to woman. Having godly women for your daughter to share her heart with and seek prayer and advice from is a huge blessing. Both my daughters have a group of older women they trust and are comfortable talking with anytime, anywhere. What a gift!

But the village does have rules. Relationships need to be treated with respect. Specifically, we can't question our daughters or members of the village about the content of discussions. And we can't be setting up our friends to gather information about things that our girls won't talk to us about. Trust is a non-negotiable if these relationships are going to work. That said, a key component of that trust is the understanding that if something is going on that presents a danger physically, emotionally or spiritually to your daughter, those trusted ladies will challenge her and hold her accountable and point her back to you (the mom) when appropriate.

I have one dear friend who has had such conversations with girls she is mentoring. It might sound like this: "I don't like this situation you're involved with. It's wrong. I'm going to give you 24 hours to talk with your parents. If you don't within 24 hours, I will."

I'm so thankful that I have women in my life who love me enough to love my daughters, too. Women who work alongside me to bring my girls into adulthood. Who show them good ways to live under authority. Who help them curb their drive to control and manipulate. Who model modesty. Who help drain any mean spiritedness. Who console tender hearts when bullied. Who speak truth to fragile egos about real beauty.

FRUIT

Since the day of their birth, I've been burdened for my daughters. In a good way. My greatest desire is for my girls to know God. To know Scripture. To radiate Jesus' love for others. To stand strong in their faith.

My girls have known since their earliest days that church is a priority. We talk regularly of God's goodness and mercy. We call out to Him – together – in times of trouble. Still, I often wonder who these girls will be when I'm not around leading them. How will they transition to the full independence of womanhood? Did I study them enough to know how to guide and shape them? Did we have enough meaningful conversations for them to develop confidence and feel secure? Is their faith truly real?

I received an answer to these questions not long ago. My daughter and I were invited to pray at her baccalaureate service. I was really worried about her. Would she know what to say? Would it be sincere? Did she want to practice? Okay, maybe these questions were really more about my fears. But as we talked, she confidently told me she was fine. No worries. But I wasn't so sure.

When the time came, I prayed first. It was…okay. Then it was my daughter's turn. As she stepped to the podium, she looked out upon her classmates, bowed her head, and spoke an eloquent, sincere, heartfelt, God-honoring prayer. It brought a tear to my eye – truly. It was not just her words that touched me, but her confident faith and conversational prayer. She was relaxed, yet bold. I was blown away. In those special moments I realized my daughter had stepped into her own. My years of giving her life were now being reciprocated and I received from her. That day brought a change in how I view her, and how I pray for her. No longer do I pray she becomes a woman of God. I pray that He protects her and equips her to live the rich and wonderful life of biblically authentic womanhood that she has embraced.

Just like my prayers needed alteration for my oldest daughter, my expectations were about to change as my other daughter entered high school. I was so excited for her to make a lot of new friends, date nice guys and immerse herself in all the things that promise to make high school special. I kept waiting. And waiting. And waiting. But the gang of friends didn't come. Neither did the guys. My expectations for her found little fulfillment. Why?

Because my dreams for her didn't align with who she is. That was hard for me to accept. Sure, she had a few close friends. But she never dated, and steered clear of the traditional trappings of high school relational drama. This made me question things about her, and about myself. It broke my heart to see her home reading on a Saturday night when I knew most kids were out with friends. It was painful for me.

But my pain wasn't justified. I was making this all about me, much like I did with my fears over my daughter's public prayer. I should have recognized that my daughter wasn't like other kids. She is certainly an amazing young lady. She knows what's right and doesn't compromise her integrity by being in the wrong place at the wrong time. She's not drawn into shallow relationships, but chooses instead the often weary road of waiting for a decent guy to date. I am so proud of her. God spared her the pain of many of the tangled webs of adolescence. She has grown into an amazing young woman of God. Now, rather than mourn what I think was lost, I regularly thank God for protecting her. For putting a hedge around her. I'm grateful that He is much wiser than me.

It's wonderful to reach this season of raising my girls and taste more fruit from my labor. To celebrate the women they are becoming. To look at them more often as peers, than children. It's not an easy transition. But then nothing about being a mom really is.

THEY SAID IT WOULD BE THIS WAY

Maybe your biggest worry today is the baby food crusted to the cupboards. Or the reality that your precious little girl, lolling off to sleep in your lap, just blew her breakfast up her back and out the leg holes of her last onesie. Cell phones and dating and emotional drama may seem a long way off. But whether you're in the season of one-item to-do lists (keep children alive) or sweating out talks of training bras and hormones, trust the oft-quoted wisdom that the teenage years will be upon you before you know it. A friend of mine, who's a father of twelve, once told me, "In raising children, the days often drag on but the years fly by." I've come to understand what he means. The speed of life is tied to events, and events increase as our kids get older. The busyness only accelerates as your daughter becomes more independent. And with rapid acceleration looms an impending collision.

I remember the meltdown. One of us got the time wrong. And there I was, sitting in yet another parking lot. I rushed to get there on time, or so I thought. Now I wasn't sure what time I was to pick her up. Twenty minutes into the waiting, I was frustrated. Ever feel like you're drowning in the carpool of life? Driving to and fro, hauling kids from one end of the city to another? It's fast food and emotional flashpoints as conversation comes in disjointed bits and pieces. But you know what? We're still talking, my daughters and me. And that's good.

In the teen years, strings of attachment loosen through every mile of taxiing my girls around. Now, I'm almost beyond the carpooling days. And trust me when I say this: I'll miss them when they're gone. Sitting in a parking lot waiting can bring comfort. For one, it's a chance for me to rest. To quiet my spirit and pray for my daughter. I pray for her safety, her friend choices, her relationships, her every coming and going. Also, in those moments of waiting, I'm comforted knowing exactly where my girl is, who she is with, and for the most part, what she's doing. And that soon we'll be together again.

All too quickly we exit the cave of diapers and crayons and tumble headlong into crazy schedules. We zip around to retrieve kids here, drop them off there, text them reminders and race home – only to head back out for another commitment. We trade waiting for naptime for waiting in the parking lot for waiting at the front window. I used to watch for her to climb off the school bus. Now I watch for headlights to turn into the driveway.

In all seasons remember: keep the balance – for you, and your daughter. Shape her mind. Help her say "no" to good things and "yes" to better things. Make home a good place to be. Help her find satisfaction and rest and value in Jesus. In the midst of our minivan parades, don't miss the small glimmers of light. The chance to snatch moments of refreshment and bits of blessing that fall from the Father of Lights.

The booger bars are gone too soon.

LETTING LOOSE

From cell phones to carpools, I face constant reminders that my girls are growing up. And so am I. My role as mom changes as they do – from generate to study to guide to engage. My teenage girls need me in different ways than just a few years ago, but they still need me.

One thing they need is for me to let go. To loosen my grip. Yes, this season of staying engaged means just that: stay engaged. But I must begin the loosening process as my girls move toward independent living. Toward being wives and homemakers and professionals… maybe even mothers. And as I let go, I pray more than ever. I pray daily for protection, for traveling mercies, for strength, for wisdom. It's a way to continue giving life to them.

I'm so proud of both my daughters. They are becoming secure and confident young women. Yet, there's still a piece of me that longs to get a call in the middle of the day and hear, "Mom, where you? I'm waiting for you!"

GIVING OUR DAUGHTERS MORE – SEASON 4

1. Don't be afraid of technology. Embrace it. Learn it. Talk about it. Monitor it. It's not going away and pretending it might won't help. Set expectations and guidelines for your teen so she's clear on boundaries and consequences.

2. Adapt your communication style as your kids mature. The way you connected when they were young may no longer work as they grow up. But don't give up. Try something until you find what works.

3. Guide your daughter toward Godly women she can connect with on a personal level. Encourage her to get involved in a small group, volunteer at Christian-based organizations, seek out teachers who follow Jesus. Look for opportunities that will foster safe, Godly relationships your daughter can pursue when she feels she can't (or doesn't want to) come to you.

4. Pray. Ask God to give you insight into your daughter's life. To hear her heart. To love her as she morphs into the amazing woman God has created her to be. Tell your daughter often how precious, loved and valuable she is – regardless of what she's wearing, her mood, or how you both are feeling in the moment.

Season 05: Hands-Off

Age 18+

Author: Julie Pearson

Julie is ever grateful for God's love and patient pursuit. She and her husband, Don, have three grown children, a son-in-law and three grandchildren who have stolen their hearts. Julie has degrees from Moody Bible Institute and Cornerstone University, and has served in ministry as a pastor's wife for 26 years. God's Word is her greatest treasure.

GOODBYE

For weeks it had been like this. Boxes, double and triple stacked all over the family room, draped with mounds of hanging clothes, bedding and towels. Finally, the morning arrived when we could cram everything into the trunks and seats of three different vehicles. My husband and I were escorting our oldest daughter to college. For years I had been dreading this day. For months the lump in my throat stubbornly arrived at the strangest moments. But the time had come. Today. Now.

I moved numbly through the events — parent orientation, roommate introductions, room set-up — trying to drum up excitement for my daughter's new adventure while keeping my emotions in check. But at our final goodbye, I lost it. Tears exploded like a canon. It was the "ugly cry." You know it. The kind where your emotions are raw and unbridled and your face is contorted beyond recognition. That flood of tears continued throughout the whole journey home – all 11 miles.

I was a complete mess and my daughter was attending a college right in our hometown!

The very next fall brought a repeat event with daughter number two. Same hometown college. Same emotional build-up. Same ugly cry.

Now before you write me off, let me say that I did pay my "far away college" dues. Two years after daughter number two, my son chose a university 13 hours away. And yep, you guessed it. Same emotional build-up. My third ugly cry.

Some of you relate to my emotional meltdowns in these transitions, others do not. I have a friend who dearly loves her son, but couldn't wait for his college departure. No tears were shed. She hugged him and said, "See ya! Don't let the door hit you on the way out!"

Clearly, we will have varying responses as our daughters transition to adulthood. And our girls will be walking many different roads. So let's be honest. We are blessed if our tears are caused by a simple college "goodbye." Perhaps your heart breaks with the weight of your daughter's foolish choices. You may be aching from a strained or non-existent relationship. Or watching your daughter battle addictions, health struggles, a learning disorder, loneliness or depression. Some of our girls are walking with God, some have strayed far from His loving arms, and some have never yet found His mercy and grace. As for us moms, we may have a supportive husband alongside us. Or we may be "going it alone."

No matter your circumstance, one thing is the same for all of us. As our girls enter the adult world, we enter a new stage of parenting. We've arrived at the cutting of those apron strings that have been stretching tighter and tighter through the high school years. Although there is no "one size fits all" approach, four centering principles can guide us as we develop our new, 'hands-off' strategies:

- Release
- Surrender
- Pray
- Be Authentic

RELEASE

Whether we welcome or resist the idea, our first task as moms of adult daughters is to become experts at fully letting go. At this stage in our parenting journey, 'release' should not be a new consideration. Most of us have been working toward this goal for years, loosening our grip bit by bit. But as our daughters reach adulthood, we've come to the point of urgency and finality.

I've discovered there are two facets to the process of letting go – outward actions and inner reality. I am learning – slowly and too often the hard way – to adjust my actions and responses in this stage of parenting. To listen instead of getting involved. To let the chips fall and not clean them up. To choke back the advice I'm bursting to give. To step back and give my daughters space and independence. To refuse to enable unhealthy choices. To invite relationship without demanding it.

These are valuable skills, every one of them necessary as we enter this new season. Yet many times my inner reality doesn't match my outward response. I might temporarily succeed at holding back my onslaught of advice. But what do I do when my mind is racing in turmoil – carrying burdens that are not mine to bear, problem solving for situations I am not involved with, worrying about things over which I have no control?

I know I am not alone in this struggle. As women, we have an urge to control. One of the biggest reasons is that we fear vulnerability. We don't want to be hurt. And when our relationships don't go well, it hurts. In fact, it can be excruciating.

When painful things happen to those we love, we ache with them. When we see our children going in the wrong direction, we fear for them. Our love makes us vulnerable, so we grasp at some measure of control to minimize the damage. And in our grasping, we put ourselves in the place of God.

To navigate this season well, we must come to terms with the fact that we are not in control of our daughters' lives. We never really were. We may have had some authority over their behavior through consequences, boundaries and limits. Yet despite our best efforts to study our girls and guide them into things truly life-giving, we never really have control. We can't manipulate their hearts or control their choices. And in adulthood, the choices are many and the stakes are higher. As moms who are wired to love and protect, how do we truly release that desire for control, even if it's just an illusion?

SURRENDER

For our release to be authentic – inside and out – it must be combined with true surrender. True surrender means that we place our daughters in God's hands, and leave them there. This isn't possible if we glue our gaze to the world our girls are living in, or their circumstances, uncertainties and struggles. We can only let go when we lift our eyes to soak in the character of God.

> *I lift up my eyes to the hills – where does my help come from? My help comes from the Lord, the Maker of heaven and earth. Psalm 121:1,2*

> *One thing God has spoken, two things have I heard: that you, O God, are strong, and that you, O Lord, are loving. Psalm 62:11,12*

These verses are my life-line. I couldn't surrender anything to God if He was strong but not loving, or loving but not strong. But because He is both strong and loving, all my bottom-line questions are answered. He is worthy of my trust.

If you need some comfort and reassurance of God's presence and power, bask in the truth of Isaiah 40:21-31. Here are just a few phrases: *He sits enthroned above the circle of the earth… He will not grow tired or weary, and His understanding no one can fathom.*

God is good. He is loving. He is strong. He is ruling the universe, and He never grows weary. Paula Rinehart says it well, "There is a world of comfort in the sovereignty of God – like the shade of a huge oak tree you can lean your tired soul upon."[6]

Lean back in the shade of God's sovereignty. And lift your eyes.

LIFTING MY EYES

I lift my eyes often these days. Remember my meltdown after taking my daughter to college in the same town? Even as I write, she is currently teaching for a year in a remote Mexican village. I recall when she first told us about the invitation she received to teach in a children's shelter. I would like to say that I "lifted my eyes," but in reality a vice-grip clenched my stomach. Fear. Worry. Uncertainty. What if she decided to go? Would she be safe? Where would she get the money? How could she even *think* about giving up a good job with insurance benefits, especially in today's economy?

My husband and I were in the car when she called to ask us to pray about this opportunity. We were on our way to the Colorado Rocky Mountains for a camping getaway. Choking back my fears, I assured her of our prayers for God's guidance and we continued our journey west. For the next ten days, I met with the Lord each morning. Bible on my lap, coffee in my hand, I lifted my eyes to the hills – literally. It was breathtaking. And as I lifted my eyes day after day, my perspective slowly changed. Staring at those majestic mountains, a confidence in God's power grew stronger than any fear for my daughter's vulnerability. His vast resources loomed larger than her need for money or a future job. Concern for those needy children in Mexico began to displace some of my worries. The possibility that God might be calling my daughter to meet that need actually brought some twinges of excitement to my heart. My Heavenly Father gently and graciously brought me to the place of inner surrender, giving me His peace as I lifted my eyes to the hills.

The greatest way to empower our daughters is by entrusting them to our God. It has been a long journey of giving life. We've birthed and studied and shaped and guided. We've sacrificed for our daughters, investing so much of our hearts and lives. Yet none of this entitles us to control or "hold on" to them as they step into adulthood. We have one more sacrifice to make on their behalf. We release. We surrender – completely.

But that is far from easy.

My friend has a daughter who has walked away from her faith. She was brought up knowing the truth of God's Word and accepted Christ as her Savior. But in her college years she threw it all away, along with her purity. She is living far from the Lord, and far from home. I asked my friend how she lifts her eyes. Here's what she said:

> *"When my own daughter walked away from God it was heartbreaking. I just wanted God to promise me that this was all going to turn out well, and to tell me how long it would take. But over time, waiting for things to change has progressed to waiting on God – and God alone. Taking my eyes off the circumstances has relieved much of the stress and allowed me to move forward in faith. I am better able to cooperate with God to see what He wants to do in my life during this time. It has also given me freedom to love and pray for my daughter, and then rest in the knowledge that God is continually at work in her life. I am clinging with a tenacious trust to the truths that God is in control, is thoroughly aware and is already working out His ultimate purposes. There is such freedom when the future depends on God instead of me. I don't understand why things have happened the way they have and I don't know how everything is going to turn out. But I know God is sovereign, He is always good and we are always loved by Him. And that is enough."*

How do we reach this place – of knowing that He is enough? How do we surrender our precious daughters when they struggle with serious health issues? When they battle depression or eating disorders? When they are cutting themselves or addicted to drugs or alcohol? When they yearn for a husband but remain single? When they get pregnant outside of marriage, or terminate the pregnancy through abortion? What if they bring home a lesbian partner? How do we surrender them when they go through a painful divorce? When they experience the pain of infertility or the loss of a child?

Thankfully, the answer is the same. Always. We lift our eyes to the hills. We focus on God's character, because it's the one thing that never changes. *"And we know that in all things God works for the good of those who love Him, who have been called according to His purpose."* (Romans 8:28) We may not understand His methods, but we can trust His character. We can trust His heart.

SIX STATEMENTS

That's why, four years ago, I wrote six statements of faith in my journal. I was struggling to surrender a situation with one of my daughters. I would lay it down, then pick it back up. Set it aside, then grab hold again. That cycle needed to end, so I put a stake in the ground. I formalized, in writing, my belief and commitment to truth. Here are those statements:

- The urgency that I feel and the need to get involved and control through pressure are not from God.

- The Creator of the ends of the earth is in control. He is at work. (Isaiah 40:21-31)

- God wants me to trust His power enough to rest, wait, and watch Him work.

- God wants me to trust His goodness and sovereignty enough to be at peace if things don't work out as I hoped.
- God wants me to hear His words, *"Be still and know that I am God."* (Psalm 46:10)
- God is the only sure foundation. The one who trusts in Him will not be dismayed. (Isaiah 28:16)

I have returned to these statements of truth again and again over the last four years. The worries of the world are relentless. We must push back with truth. All day. Every day.

PRAY

With release and surrender, we leave the active playing field of parenting and take our place on the sidelines. But as we do, our life-giving role as mothers does not diminish. We do not retire. In fact the paradox of this season is that, as our daughters leave, our power and influence can grow. We have the privilege of pouring out truth and blessings on them until the day we die – through our prayers.

In recent years I've been learning much about prayer. And prayer always changes our hearts. So I have a confession. I am seeing that the desires I have for my children aren't always the best.

My youngest daughter is currently single. Without realizing it, at the top of my praying 'wish list' was the desire for her to have a godly man. A man she could walk through life with. A man who would love and cherish her, be faithful to her, and partner with her in serving God. I have no doubt that marriage is God's good plan. He said it wasn't good for man to be alone. And it's great to pray for my daughter to be joined to a good man. But it's not the best desire I could have for her.

Whether or not my wish comes true, a greater thing is happening in my daughter's time of singleness. She's learning that God is enough – even when she's lonely. She's finding deeper joy in her walk with God. She's understanding more of His intimate love for her. She's exploring and discovering who God made her to be and how she can best serve Him and bring Him glory. She's identifying the sinful lies she's believed about herself and how to fight for God's truth. What a gift!

At the other end of the spectrum is my oldest daughter. She's a mom with three young children. She dearly loves her husband and treasures her little ones. But I remember well the demands of that season. Sometimes I see the struggle in her eyes or hear it in her voice, and I take on the burden of her weariness. My thoughts start swirling, trying to come up with ways to relieve her stress or make things better. I find myself desiring — at times, more than anything else — that she be stress-free and happy.

But a greater thing is happening to her as I watch and pray. She's in the process of learning the painfully beautiful secret of dying to self, setting aside her desires to meet the needs of her children. She's wrestling with goals and struggling to live by priorities. She's coming to grips with the 'keep children alive' to-do list. She's getting fresh glimpses of her sinful tendencies that flare up under stress and crying out to God for help. She has a heightened awareness of her need for His unending resources. God is at work in her life in wonderful, eternal ways that I would have totally missed had I stayed focused on my desire for her to be stress-free and happy. My daughter is learning what it means to simplify and give life.

Two daughters. Different circumstances. But the same tension for me – to look beyond my own desires for them as I release and surrender and pray. To let God help me reassess what is best, in light of His greater purposes. To take my hands off so my daughters can flourish.

PATTERNS

We all need help to look beyond the immediate circumstances in our daughter's lives so we can see where God is at work. Then we can join Him through prayer. When we pray with spiritual eyes, we can trust that God is working behind the scenes in the most important ways, even if the circumstances don't change immediately. Even if the circumstances don't change – ever.

Realizing that I needed help with my prayers, I began to pattern them after the prayers in the Bible, especially the prayers of the apostle Paul. Ephesians 1:17-18 is one of my favorites: *"I keep asking that the God of our Lord Jesus Christ, the glorious Father, may give you the Spirit of wisdom and revelation, so that you may know him better. I pray also that the eyes of your heart may be enlightened in order that you may know the hope to which he has called you…"*

Here's another: *"I pray that you…may have power…to grasp how wide and long and high and deep is the love of Christ, and to know this love that surpasses knowledge – that you may be filled to the measure of all the fullness of God."* (Ephesians 3:18-19)

What amazing spiritual insight and eternal vision. My mind is being renewed and my perspective is changing – not only for my daughters, but also for myself. In this new season, we can continue to pour out life through our prayers. Prayer is a powerful weapon, and we can have full confidence that we're praying for God's will if we are praying His words.

*(*More passages to pray for your daughter are listed at the end of this chapter.)*

God is so good. He knows just what we need. He has given us prayer as an outlet for our worry and fear. *"Do not be anxious about anything, but in everything, by prayer and petition, with thanksgiving, present your requests to God. And the peace of God, which transcends all understanding, will guard your hearts and your minds in Christ Jesus."* (Philippians 4:6-7).

Over and over, these verses have been water to my parched soul. I am a worrier and I have many fears. But this is where I take them. This is where I lay them down. This is where I go, again and again, until His peace begins to guard my heart and mind. Until I hear His voice whispering, *"Be still, and know that I am God."* (Psalm 46:10)

BE AUTHENTIC

Authenticity is another powerful weapon of influence we can wield from the sidelines. Though we may have less opportunity to verbally speak into the adult lives of our daughters, our actions will speak louder than words. If we continue growing in God's truth – and live it out – our daughters *will* be impacted.

But how do we live authentically? Where do we start? We start by discovering who or what we worship. Sadly, for me this is sometimes different than who I say I worship, or who I know I *should* worship. My life always tells the truth when I take the time to examine it. What do I think about the most? How do I spend the majority of my discretionary time, or my money?

So many things vie for our passions and focus: money, comfort, food, fitness, clothes, decor, professional pursuits, friends, romance. The list is endless. And if we're not careful, our children (and grand-children) can steal that position of primary focus. Dr. Larry Crabb has said it so well:

> *Put your children's well-being at the center of your life, and you burden them with a responsibility their shoulders were never designed to carry. When parents' joy finally depends upon their children doing well and relating warmly to mom and dad, they become idolaters.*
>
> *C.S. Lewis wrote, "Put first things first and second things are thrown in. Put second things first and you lose both first and second things."*
>
> *The first thing — what the gospel guarantees, what our soul desperately needs and wants — is not a well-adjusted, happy child. The first thing is God, access to Him, the enjoyment of relationship with Him even if all other relationships fall apart and leave us in agonizing pain. The first thing is worship, the freedom and power to live for God in any circumstance and to love God no matter how broken our hearts might be. Everything else is a second thing.*
>
> *We must resist the strong tendency to let our ultimate joy depend on how our children are doing or on how they relate with us. We must make sure we're worshipping God, not worshipping our children and asking them to fill our hearts as only God can do.*[7]

This is much-needed truth throughout our parenting journey, but it's perhaps even more crucial for this last season. If our children are the center of our lives, we won't be able to release and surrender in a healthy way. The empty hole will be too great. And rather than be empty, we'll contrive ways to manipulate and control and hang on. If the children are our first priority, we are seeking a false identity built on a very shaky foundation.

TRANSITIONS

Times of transition – like releasing in parenting – are a gift to me. Not like a birthday gift. I'm never eager to receive the gift of transition because I don't like change – at all. For me, change brings a host of unsettling emotions. The 'gift' part comes when I'm forced to take inventory and realign my heart and my life with God. To make Him my first thing. Whenever I look back, I am thankful. But in the moment, it can be messy and uncomfortable.

We can't let go of something without filling that place with something else. Some of us have been waiting since childbirth for the day when we can finally have more "me time." Some of us are so enmeshed in our children's lives we wouldn't have a clue what to do with "me time." No matter our perspective, authentic living demands intentional thought and planning.

Our walk with God must take first place. If there was ever a doubt about this, Jesus settled it (Matthew 22:36-40). What's most important? To love God with all our heart, soul, mind and strength. To daily soak in His truth as we read His Word, the Bible. To let it fill our thoughts as we meditate on it. To talk with Him in prayer, asking Him to expand our love for Him and for others. To let His Kingdom values take root in our hearts and spill out through our actions.

God's Word is living and active. As it penetrates our hearts, we will be changed. And that's wonderful news. We have continuing opportunities for growth and change in this new season.

The Lord has broken down two strongholds in my life in recent years. And I do mean strongholds. One was a long-standing lie I believed that caused me to live in a place of constant defeat, robbing me of joy. The second was an idol, a false god I had used to try to fill the emptiness. But I was in bondage, and all attempts to break free were futile until God's truth finally took root.

Though these areas are still works in progress, I have been able to share these breakthroughs with my family and enlist their prayers for continued strength and victory. I'm sad that my children had to witness my sin all these years. I'm sad for the ways it has hurt my husband. But I'm praying that the power of God shines even brighter in the midst of my great weakness. That's the great news about living authentically. We don't have to hide. We don't have to pretend. We just need to keep walking on with our Savior, letting Him lead and trusting His work in us.

I share these victories with greatest humility. I know how stuck I was. I give all the glory to God. But I share them to encourage anyone who has given up hope. God is continually at work in our lives. If we persevere in making Him our highest passion and fill ourselves with His truth, we will be changed. Our lives will affirm how great He is, and how worthy He is of all our love.

This is number one. And it's non-negotiable for authentic lives.

If married, our husbands are next in priority. The best gift we can give our children, at any age, is a good marriage. And we know this takes effort and intentional planning.

My husband and I recently had one of those long, power talks. It was tension-filled and messy. He was pointing out that our marriage had slipped down on the priority list. Sounding the alarm so that we could put out the competing fires and get back in sync with each other. At first I was defensive and angry. Accusations and justifications welled up inside me. But I knew I couldn't camp out here, and I knew where to take it. Straight to God, begging for His help. And as my vision cleared, I saw that my husband was right. He was on *my* team, and we wanted the *same* things.

And so, once again, we asked forgiveness for the ways we had hurt each other. We talked and planned and regrouped. We asked God for help in protecting and nurturing our marriage, and in balancing all of the demands of life. We affirmed our desire to love better, deeper, fuller.

Authentic living. It doesn't require perfection but it does require courage – courage to see ourselves as we truly are. And when we uncover our brokenness, we take that to God so that He can keep moving us forward, conforming us to His image, making us more beautiful.

TRUE BEAUTY

"A woman of true beauty is a woman who in the depths of her soul is at rest, trusting God because she has come to know him to be worthy of her trust. She exudes a sense of calm, a sense of rest, and invites those around her to rest as well. She speaks comfort; she knows that we live in a world at war, that we have a vicious enemy, and our journey is through a broken world. But she also knows that because of God all is well, that all will be well. A woman of true beauty offers others the grace to be and the room to become." [8]

The grace to be and the room to become. Precious gifts, indeed. If we can offer these gifts to our daughters, wrapped in prayer and framed in authentic lives, we will be passing on the greatest of treasures.

He will be the sure foundation for your times, a rich store of salvation and wisdom and knowledge; the fear of the Lord is the key to this treasure. (Isaiah 33:6)

GIVING OUR DAUGHTERS MORE – SEASON 5

1. Become an expert listener. Instead of jumping in to control or problem solve, just listen. Step back to give your daughter space and independence. If this is especially hard for you, adopt the "24-hour rule": *I will not do or say anything with regard to this situation for 24 hours.* Then pray, surrender it to the Lord, seek His wisdom.

2. Rest in God so you can stop rescuing. Place your daughter in God's hands and stand firm on that foundation. Refuse to enable unhealthy choices. Let the chips fall – and don't clean them up. The 24-hour rule may be helpful again here, giving you the strength you need to stand firm against the emotional pull to rescue until you can see more clearly.

3. Invite relationship without demanding it. Try to be as compatible with your daughter's world as possible, rather than expecting her to adapt to yours. This will require making peace with her schedule and with her preferred method of communication - without taking it personally. If she never returns your phone calls but texts you back within minutes, text her whenever possible. If she rarely checks her email but lives on Facebook, message her there instead. Warmly invite relationship, but don't demand it.

4. Pour out truth and blessings on your daughter through praying God's Word.

Romans 15:13

2 Corinthians 13:14

Ephesians 1:16-20

Ephesians 3:14-19

Philippians 1:3-6

Philippians 1:9-11

Colossians 1:9-12

Colossians 4:12

1 Thessalonians 3:12-13

2 Thessalonians 2:16-17

2 Thessalonians 3:5

Conclusion

Take a moment and pause. Who are the women in your story who have brought something to life within you? Think about the women you most admire for the way they live out their femininity – those who relate with softness yet strength, truth yet encouragement. Who stepped in with wisdom when you were in need of guidance?

Savor those faces. Their input in your story is allowing you to shape the life of your daughter. Allowing you to give her more than plastic-coated femininity.

Whose face comes to *my* mind? A lady with a three-inch, three-ring binder detailing all the categories needed to plan a wedding successfully. Maps, store hours, receipts, calendar, and the phone number of a talented dress seamstress. But when I stood before her on my wedding day, she didn't hold up the binder, wink and say, "We did it! We planned a snazzy wedding!" Instead, I stood on my wedding day, secure in my station in life because she had spent the last 26 years attending to my feminine soul.

That is what lasts.

I can picture my mom, as she blazed a rebel trail through natural childbirth practices so that she might give her baby girl an optimum first cry. She was *generating* life for me from the very start.

On my first day of kindergarten, she rode the school bus with me so she could see the route and listen to the conversations on the bus and hold my hand – all while carrying a 13-pound (not an exaggeration) nine-month-old baby in her womb. She was intent on *studying* me and my world.

In middle school, despite my eye-rolling and huffing and puffing, my mom still attended the eternally awkward "what's happening to your body" class the public school offers, because knowing how the school addresses puberty was important. More important than being liked by her daughter. She knew it was her primary responsibility to *guide* me, not the school's. She courageously and persistently *engaged* with my heart and with my life.

Even during the *hands-off* years of college she found ways to love and support me. Do you remember how you felt when you and your boyfriend broke up? Me too. Like I might never breathe again. And my mom drove to my out-of-state college for the weekend, just to take me out for dinner and bring me homemade cookies and Kleenex boxes.

I long to give my daughters all that my mom has poured into me. To generate sustaining, life-giving qualities in their heart. To develop their minds. Celebrate true beauty. Encourage softness. Instill confidence. And together, enjoy our God-breathed, feminine stamp.

God has designed our daughters with unique, inner beauty and He has equipped us, as moms, to draw it out. This ability is *yours* – to generate life, touch hearts and powerfully influence – in every season.

There are no guarantees. In the end, our daughters must choose whether they will walk with God or chart their own course. But we pray and hold tightly to hope, knowing that God will never stop loving them or pursuing their hearts. And He will go ahead of you – and me – leading the way, filling us up so we can give more to our daughters than we ever thought possible.

And God is able to make all grace abound to you, so that in all things, at all times, having all that you need, you will abound in every good work. (2 Corinthians 9:8)

Endnotes

[1] David G. Myers, *Exploring Psychology*, (New York: Worth Publishers, 2011), 139

[2] Annie Sullivan, *The Story of My Life* by Helen Keller, 1903

[3] C.S. Lewis, *Mere Christianity*, (New York: MacMillan Company, 1952), 100

[4] Leonard Sax, *Girls On The Edge*, (New York: Basic Books, 2010), 12

[5] Sax, *Girls on The Edge*, 12

[6] Paula Rinehart, *Better Than My Dreams*, (Nashville: Thomas Nelson, 2007), 99

[7] From the writings of Dr. Larry Crabb, http://www.newwayministries.org

[8] John and Stasi Eldredge, *Captivating*, (Nashville: Thomas Nelson, 2005), 135